Spiders

NATURE'S PREDATORS

Stuart A. Kallen

KidHaven Press

KidHaven Press, an imprint of Gale Group, Inc.
P.O. Box 289009, San Diego, CA 92198-9009

Library of Congress Cataloging-in-Publication Data

Kallen, Stuart A., 1955–
  Spiders / by Stuart A. Kallen.
    p. cm.—(Nature's Predators)
    Includes bibliographical references (p.).
    Summary: Discusses the habitat of spiders, their anatomy, cam-
  ouflage ability, means of catching prey, and the various types of
  spider lairs.
    ISBN 0-7377-0630-9 (hardback)
    1. Spiders—Juvenile literature. [1. Spiders.] I. Title. II
  Nature's Predators (San Diego, Calif.)
  QL458.4 .K345 2002
  595.4'4—dc21

  00-012810

Copyright 2002 by KidHaven Press, an imprint of Gale Group, Inc.
P. O. Box 289009, San Diego, CA 92198-9009

Contents

Chapter 1

The Efficient Killer

Most spiders are less than two inches long. The largest ones are not much bigger than a human hand. But large or small, spiders are some of the most skillful **predators** in the world. Stalking their prey with eight long legs, poisonous venom, and sticky silk, spiders spend their lives hunting, killing, and eating.

Spiders have been excellent predators for almost 400 million years. And the leggy creatures are found almost everywhere, from dark, dusty basements to caves, ponds, and forests.

There are more than thirty-five thousand different kinds, or **species**, of spiders. They can be found on every continent except Antarctica. Taken together, there are billions and billions of spiders on the planet.

The spider's body size is as varied as its **habitat**. The smallest spiders from the Anapidae family measure .02 inches—smaller than the head of a pin. These tiny creatures live on the South Sea island of Samoa and eat moss and microscopic organisms. The largest spider is the giant South American bird-eating tarantula. Its body measures up to three and a half inches long, and its legs stretch out ten inches.

While the flower spider (pictured) is small enough to fit on a flower's stem, there are other spiders that are even smaller.

The South American tarantula can grow to be up to three and a half inches long.

Spider Bodies

Although spiders are sometimes referred to as insects, they are not. Insects have only six legs, but spiders have eight. Most insects have wings and antennae, which spiders do not have.

An insect's body has three parts, a head, a **thorax**, and an **abdomen**. Spiders' bodies, however, have only two parts, an abdomen and a **cephalothorax**, the upper body part that combines the head and the thorax into a single section. This segment of the spider's body is protected

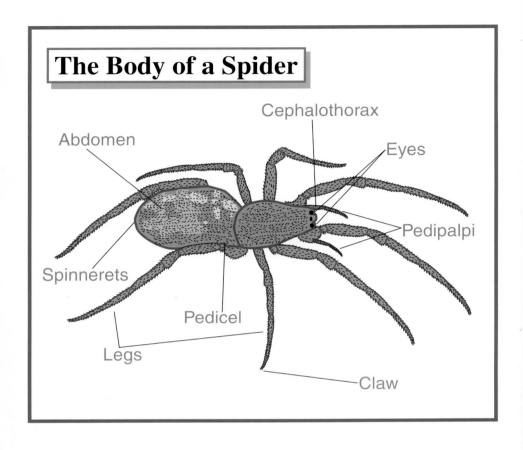

The Body of a Spider

Cephalothorax

Abdomen

Eyes

Pedipalpi

Spinnerets

Pedicel

Legs

Claw

by a hard shell, known as the **carapace**, which is similar to a crab shell.

Attached to the cephalothorax are four pairs of legs. Each of these eight legs has seven joints. This means that a spider has fifty-six knees, and if it accidentally loses a leg, it can grow a new one.

About two-thirds of spider species have four pairs of eyes, or eight eyes. The rest have only three or two pairs of eyes. Spiders that live in the dark, such as the cave spider, have no eyes at all.

The arrangement of the eyes differs from species to species. Since each type of spider has a different eye display, these variations are used to identify and classify spiders.

The Hungry Spider

Spiders are meat eaters, or **carnivores**. Most species eat live insects that are common to their environment. The largest spiders, such as tarantulas, have big appetites, sometimes eating small mice, birds, or snakes. Wood spiders build webs that are so strong that they can sometimes ensnare bats or small birds.

A spider devours its prey, which is as large as he is.

Some spiders are cannibals, eating other species of spiders and even their own kind. Female Araneus spiders eat their partners after they mate. And when baby Coelotes spiders are born, they may eat their mother if she does not escape.

No matter what their **prey**, spiders can live for long periods of time without eating. If food is scarce, spiders can live weeks, or even months, with no food.

How the Spider Got Its Name

Spiders belong to the **Arthropoda** family of the animal kingdom. Arthropods consist of creatures with segmented bodies and pairs of jointed legs. Spiders are arachnids (uh-RACK-nids), a segment of the Arthropoda family.

The word *spider* comes from the Old English term *spinnan*, which means "to spin," referring to the webs that spiders weave. The term *arachnid* comes from an ancient Greek legend about a girl named Arachne who won a weaving contest with the goddess Athena. According to the legend, Athena became angry at Arachne's superior weaving skills and hit the young girl in front of the crowd that had gathered to watch the contest. Arachne was humiliated and killed herself. Athena then took pity on Arachne and brought her back to life as a web-weaving spider.

Amazing Silk

Like Arachne, spiders are amazing weavers. They make webs from a sticky threadlike substance called silk that is produced inside their bodies by silk glands. Spiders make up to five kinds of silk. One type is used for webs, another for hunting, and others to protect baby spider eggs or build shelters.

A spider squeezes out silk from small tubes called **spinnerets** on the abdomen. The silk is a sticky liquid that hardens into a strong thread when exposed to the air. As it dries, small finger-like projections on the spinnerets shape the silk into various shapes.

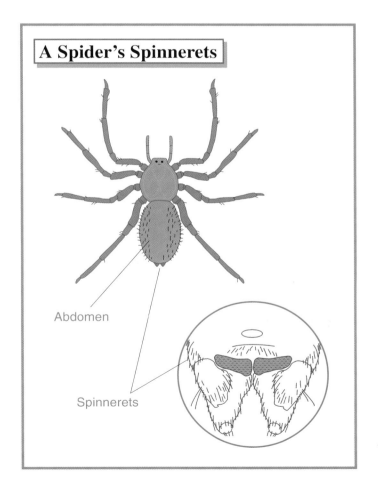

A Spider's Spinnerets

Abdomen

Spinnerets

Some spiders spin sticky webs of silk to trap insects.

Silk helps spiders hunt and kill their prey. Some kinds of spiders capture insects in silk webs. But not all spiders weave webs. Some use silk like a cowboy's lasso, throwing it over a victim and tying it up. Others blind and confuse their victims by shooting wads of gummy silk into their eyes. The spitting spider shoots a gob of gooey silk over a victim, gluing it to the ground where it can then be eaten.

Spider silk is extremely strong. A web will hold four thousand times the spider's weight. And silk is three times stronger than a steel thread of the same thickness. In spite of this strength, silk is extremely flexible—it can be stretched to double its length before it breaks.

Hairy Legs

Silk is an important hunting tool, but spider bodies are also efficiently designed to capture prey.

The long, thin legs of the spider are covered in hairs that are very sensitive to vibration. When an insect flutters its wings or walks by, these tiny hairs tell the spider that dinner is nearby.

Different types of body hair serve different purposes. Spiders use specialized hairs to "hear" sound vibrations because they don't have ears.

Other hairs help spiders "talk" to one another. They may rub their legs on each other or on their **palps**, jointed **appendages** on the spider's head. Spiders can also scrape their legs over a set of ridges on the abdomen, drum their palps on the surface, or vibrate appendages against each other. Some of the clicking sounds produced are similar to the noises made by crickets and grasshoppers.

These signals are used during mating rituals. A male fighting for a female will make loud

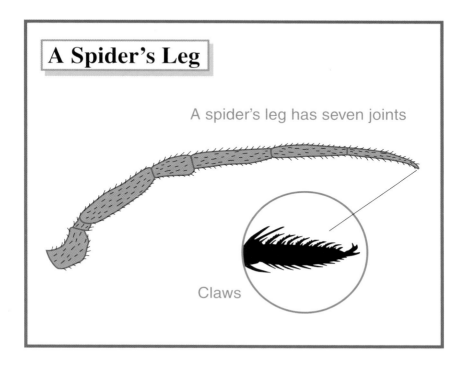

A Spider's Leg

A spider's leg has seven joints

Claws

hissing sounds to scare off other potential mates. And when a male spider approaches a female, he makes special sounds to warn of his approach so that she does not kill him as she would her prey.

Powerful Jaws

Once a spider has captured its prey, its powerful jaws go to work to kill and eat the victim. The jaws of the spider are located on the underside of the cephalothorax, along with the mouth.

Spiders' jaws work in two ways. Some spider jaws strike down against the prey with a long, pointy fang. Other species use a pincerlike jaw that impales prey on fangs that are clinched together. Once the prey is immobilized in this manner, the spider injects **venom**, or poison, into the victim to paralyze it.

Spiders can tell if a meal is edible or poisonous by the two appendages on either side of the jaw known as palps. These small organs, also called pedipalps look like two tiny legs. Palps are used by the spider to taste and smell.

Sucking up a Meal

After the fangs have injected a victim with venom, spiders use a different liquid to eat their prey. Most animals, including humans, digest food in their stomachs with the aid of digestive juices called **enzymes.** But spiders digest food outside their bodies.

Spiders' fangs shoot digestive enzymes into a creature after the venom has paralyzed it. These

A wolf spider clutches its prey, a fly.

juices slowly soften up the victim's internal organs, turning them to liquid. The spider then sucks up the liquid through its mouth using an organ called a sucking stomach. When the spider is finished with its meal, the empty husk of the insect's outer shell is left behind.

Efficient Killing Machines

Spiders have been on earth ten thousand times longer than modern humans. In that time, they have developed a wide variety of clever hunting methods. Because of its eight agile legs, numerous sets of eyes, powerful jaws, and skillful use of silk, there are few animals in the world that are as cunning and deadly as the average spider.

Chapter 2

Spiders Without Webs

Since spiders live in many different environments, each species has adopted its own way of hunting. Although many kinds of spiders use webs, a large number of species simply hide and wait for their prey to wander by. When a victim comes close, the spider jumps from its hiding place and grabs it with silk or bites it with sharp jaws.

Trap-Door Spiders

One type of spider known for its deadly fangs is the trap-door spider. To catch and kill insects, trap-door spiders dig small holes in the ground called burrows. After the hole is dug, the spider lines its new dwelling with silk and pulls a door, usually a leaf or piece of bark, into place.

To ambush its prey, the spider leaves its two front legs sticking out from under the door. The

Sensing a victim nearby, a trap-door spider prepares to ambush its prey.

tiny hairs on the trap-door's legs tell it when a victim is nearby. At the right moment, the spider leaps out and grabs the insect, killing it instantly with its large fangs. The prey is then quickly dragged down into the burrow to be eaten. After it has had its meal, the trap-door spider can wait motionless for days, or even weeks, until the next victim appears.

Ambush Methods

Some spider species, such as the *Segestria* spider, have improved the trap-door spider's methods to ambush prey. These spiders surround their burrows with many silk threads, called trip wires, that radiate outward like the spokes of a bicycle wheel. The spider hides in the burrow with its front legs on the trip wires. When a small insect scurries by, the spider feels the wires vibrate and jumps on its victim.

The spinning of silk takes energy, however, so twig-line spiders in Australia have adapted a simpler method. They do not bother to weave thread. Instead, they simply drag small twigs and other plant debris into a pattern of trip wires around their burrows.

The purse-web spider builds a burrow like a trap-door spider but uses a different method to capture prey. The spider weaves a tube, or purse, of silk extending out from the burrow. To hide the bright, white silk purse lying on the ground, the spider covers, or **camouflages**, it with dirt and leaf debris.

The spider then lies upside down inside the purse web and waits. When an unwary insect lands on the hidden tube, the purse-web spider jabs its fangs up through the silk and into the belly of the insect above. Using a special row of teeth, the spider saws through the purse and pulls the prey down into the tube. After dragging the paralyzed bug into the burrow, the spider repairs the purse and waits for the next victim.

Hiding in the Open

Another sort of ambush is practiced by spiders whose camouflage markings allow them to hide in plain view. Flower spiders are bright yellow or white. Their coloring allows them to hide within flower petals. And they can change their color between white and yellow to match whatever type of flower they are near.

When bees, butterflies, or hoverflies come to collect pollen or drink nectar from the flower, the flower spider grabs the insect with its strong front legs, kills it with venom, and eats it.

Not all flower spiders are yellow or white. The heather spider is a beautiful creature whose color allows it to hide on the pink petals of heather flowers.

Flower spiders' coloring allows them to hide within flower petals.

19

Hunting Down Prey

While flower and trap-door spiders lie in wait for their prey, other hunters aggressively search for food. Night-hunting spiders hide in the daytime in small silken lairs built under stones or pieces of tree bark. There are more than two thousand species of night hunters worldwide. Although most of them have eight small eyes, they rely on touch and smell to locate prey.

The mouse spider, whose furry brown body looks like a tiny mouse, is very common in North America. By day, mouse spiders hide in gardens under flowerpots and flagstones. At night, the spiders can be seen darting about like mice, climbing house walls searching for bugs to eat. Mouse spiders are not picky eaters. They will eat insects that have been dead for a long time such as lifeless flies lying on windowsills. And in spite of their small size, mouse spiders are mean. They have been known to give humans painful—but not deadly—bites.

Amazing Jumping Spiders

Whereas mouse spiders are fast runners, jumping spiders can leap great distances to bring down their prey.

Jumping spiders are very small—about half an inch—but they can jump seven inches, up to fourteen times their body length. Among their four pairs of eyes, jumpers have two very large

Despite being very small, jumping spiders, like this one, can leap up to seven inches.

eyes on tubes that turn and bend. Jumpers prowl the forest restlessly, turning their eye stalks in a constant search for food, seeking out flies and other flying insects.

The jaws of the jumping spiders are so strong, and their venom so potent, that they can kill bugs much larger than themselves. When a jumper spots a victim, it leaps onto its back, sinking its venomous fangs into the neck.

There are about four thousand species of jumpers worldwide. The zebra-striped jumper prowls North American backyards, perched on brick walls in search of mosquitoes and gnats that it can pluck out of the air. In Australia, the *Mopsus mormon* can be seen wrapped around dragonflies, injecting poison into their necks as the two creatures crash to the ground.

With more than four thousand species worldwide, jumping spiders can be found in places like Australia and Mount Everest.

Successful Species

Creatures such as mouse spiders and jumping spiders are some of the oldest animal species on earth. Their hunting habits have changed little in the past 100 million years. And there is little reason for change. They are incredibly successful species that have outlasted dinosaurs, wooly mammoths, and countless other creatures.

Jumping spiders have been found as high as Mount Everest, the tallest mountain in the world. Crab spiders have been seen hunting in seemingly lifeless lava beds where volcanoes had recently erupted. In fact there are few places on earth where hunting spiders cannot build a lair or find a meal.

Chapter 3

The Web Spinners

About half of all spider species build webs to catch their prey. These webs are as varied as the spiders that build them, appearing in shapes such as funnels, tubes, orbs, and scaffolds.

Webs are designed for different purposes. Some are made to catch crawling bugs, others to ensnare jumping insects. And some are built to catch flying insects or even birds. Some webs are huge, stretching five feet between trees in a forest. Others are made up of a single hanging sticky thread.

Wrapping the Prey

Once victims are caught in webs, spiders use two different methods to kill them. Some spiders use the "bite-wrap" attack. They paralyze the prey with their venom, then quickly wrap the victim in silk to carry it back to their home base. This method is dangerous, because the trapped prey might attack and injure the spider.

Other spiders stand a distance from the prey ensnared in the web and throw silk over it using the back legs. This tightly binds the prey and cuts off any means of escape. The spider then moves closer and spins the victim, laying layer after layer of silk over the body. If the prey is too large for this maneuver, the spider will simply run around the

A spider approaches prey that it has wrapped in its web.

carcass until it is wrapped. Once the prey is completely mummified in silk, the spider carefully approaches and injects it with a bite of venom.

This approach is useful against insects such as wasps and dragonflies, which will fight the spider to the death if necessary. But not all spiders will fight such powerful insects. Some species will battle a wasp. Others will gingerly cut the web around the insect to allow it to escape.

The Orb Web

Spiders weave webs of many shapes and sizes. The most familiar is the orb-shaped web. This type of web offers many advantages to the spider. The web's strength allows it to be anchored to solid objects at very few points. Because of this, the spider can build webs in many different types of places, from tree branches to the corners of rooms. And orb webs allow spiders to catch flying insects that would otherwise be out of reach.

A spider at home in its orb-shaped web waits for its prey.

How a Spider Spins an Orb Web

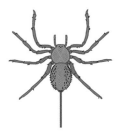

A spider drops a line, relying on a breeze to blow the free end to a resting place.

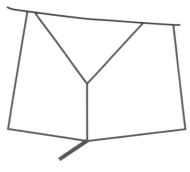

A spider then constructs a frame on which to build its web.

The orb web often covers a large area of space high off the ground. Some orbs may span less than two inches, while others extend ten feet or more. The strong yellow webs of the *Nephila,* a type of long-jawed orb weaver, can be as large as sixty feet across.

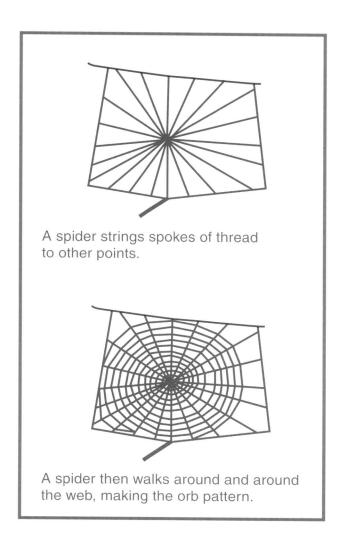

A spider strings spokes of thread to other points.

A spider then walks around and around the web, making the orb pattern.

To build an orb web, spiders lay a single basic bridge line. The spider either walks between two points or lets a breeze blow the thread from one point to another. Once it is in place, the spider strengthens the bridge by adding extra thread to it.

Next, the spider drops a loop of silk down from the bridge and anchors it at a third point. The spider may now walk out from the center point, stringing spokes of thread to other points. After this is done, it will walk around and around the web, making spirals of thread into the familiar orb pattern. Spinning a web is a lot of work for the spider, and it will only make a new web when absolutely necessary.

Hiding in the Orb

Once the orb web is finished, the spider must hide until an insect flies into its trap. Some spiders leave the web and hide near the edge. Others weave patterns similar to their bodies in the center of the web. A garden spider, for instance, weaves a thick oval crosshatched pattern of bluish silk in the center of its web. The spider sitting motionless in the center cannot be seen by unwary prey.

The three-lobed spider camouflages its orb web by placing twigs, small pieces of leaves, and dead insect skeletons in the silk. The spider looks very much like this debris and disappears behind this camouflage as it waits to pounce.

Sheet Webs and Funnels

Another common web design is the milky netting of sheet-web spiders often seen in forests and gardens. These webs are made from two silken platforms that are draped across grass or low plants. The web is not sticky, but is zigzagged with dozens of trip lines above, below, and between the sheet webs. Prey become trapped in this jumble of thread, and the spider can quickly grab a trapped insect. The prey is then pulled into a hidden lair within the web to be eaten in safety.

Sheet webs with tubular lairs at the end are called funnel webs. Funnel weavers hide in the tube and grab insects that have crashed into the web. The victims are bitten and dragged into the funnel where they can be safely eaten.

Once caught in a funnel web, victims are bitten and dragged into the funnel to be eaten.

Casting a Net

Net-casting spiders that are found in tropical climates use their webs in a unique manner. Net casters are long and very thin, and they resemble twigs. They use their four spindly front legs to hold nets to capture passing prey.

To build its trap, the net caster weaves a simple sheet web. The spider then weaves thick bands of special silk into the sheet to form a small, square web. It cuts the miniature net free and grasps the four corners between each of its elongated four front legs.

The spider waits for prey with its head down. When an insect flies by, the spider opens the web to its full size, catching the victim in the net. The spider then wraps its prey and locks it up with more silk. After eating its meal, the spider begins work on a new net.

If no flying insects are nearby, the net catcher might climb onto a low area of its sheet web and wait for a ground insect to walk by. In this case, the spider will simply drop the net over its victim, wrap up the struggling insect, and eat it.

Water Spiders

The European water spider uses its silk to hunt underwater in a pond or lake. The water spider begins by weaving a small, arched silk bell between two plants under the surface of the water. It then swims to the surface and grabs a bubble of water between its hind legs. Using its other legs, the spider swims down to the lair and releases the bubble. The air stays trapped in the silken bell. This process is repeated dozens of times until the air in the bell has expanded to the size of a thimble—large enough to fit the spider's body.

The spider waits in its lair for tiny shrimp, fish, or tadpoles to swim by. When a victim comes near, the spider throws its long silvery legs around the creature and injects venom into its neck. If the fish is large, it might be dragged to the surface to be consumed on the shore. Otherwise the prey is eaten in the spider's lair.

Water spiders may spend their entire lives underwater in their air-bubble webs. They mate within the web and lay eggs there as well.

A water spider and his air-filled lair.

The black widow is an aggressive attacker.

To add to their diets, water spiders can also swim down to the bottom of the pond and search for insect larvae or other bottom-dwelling creatures. But water spiders do not require a large diet. Their heart rate is half that of other spiders, and they need less food to survive.

Water spiders live in cold northern climates where the water freezes in the winter. When the water freezes, the spider's air-bubble lair disappears. But water spiders can survive the winter in a state of hibernation. When the ice melts, the water spider thaws, rebuilds its lair, and resumes its hunting chores.

Aggressive Behavior

Most spiders will only capture prey that they can easily kill. But some types of sheet-web spiders will fight wasps, beetles, grasshoppers, and other aggressive prey. These spiders recognize their enemies and act to neutralize their defenses.

When a wasp lands in a sheet web, the spider will immediately wrap silk around the deadly stinger on the wasp's tail end. If a spider wants to battle a beetle, silk is used to tie down the sharp, snapping jaws of the prey. The powerful kicking legs of grasshoppers are also immobilized with silk.

Some aggressive spiders go further than battling large insects. The funnel-web spider of Australia, for instance, will assault a human being. When male funnel webs are in search of a mate, they will attack humans on the slightest provocation. A bite from this spider can bring numbness and vomiting. The lungs fail and the victim might go into a coma unless quickly treated.

Advanced Spiders

Web-building spiders may be aggressive or passive. But their use of webs for hunting separates them from most other animals on earth.

Scientists believe that at one time all spiders were webless hunters. Over the eons, however, some species of spiders evolved to use their silk to weave webs. These web builders proved to be some of the world's cleverest food catchers.

While humans may use fishing poles, bows and arrows, or guns to capture prey, few other animals are able to rely on such tools. But over time, billions of spiders have learned to weave beautiful—and deadly—webs to trap and kill their prey.

Chapter 4

Fighting Off Attackers

Spiders are fierce hunters who skillfully capture, kill, and eat their prey. But they themselves are easy prey for larger animals. Spiders are considered a food source by many animals, including scorpions, lizards, frogs, possums, mice, and many types of birds.

Trap-door spiders, for example, are well protected in their burrows. The only time they leave is when it is necessary to hunt or mate. But some larger mammals, such as the Australian bandicoot, will simply dig up the ground to catch the spider in its burrow. Other animals, such as centipedes and scorpions, however, are blocked by the snug-fitting doors built by the spider. When under attack, the spider will hold the trapdoor tightly with its jaws and legs, preventing the predator from entering.

A trap-door spider can defend itself by hiding in its lair and holding down the trapdoor.

One type of Australian trap-door spider places a second trapdoor deep within the lair. If a hungry lizard tries to enter the burrow, the spider pulls the second door shut. Other spiders build forked burrows, using one fork as a home and a second tunnel as an escape route.

Camouflage

Web builders usually hide off to the sides of their webs, between leaves, or under tree bark. Sometimes they camouflage their hidden den by placing leaves, dirt, animal droppings, and even the skeletons of their victims around it. This sort of walled lair also protects the spider from the hot sun and drenching rain.

Building a camouflage lair offers the web-building spider excellent protection. Other spiders are able to hide by using the natural camouflage on their bodies and legs. These spiders sit in the open but are hard to distinguish because their patchy brown or gray bodies resemble bumps on logs, sandy soil, or other features of their habitat. The wall crab spider in Arizona has a mottled body and legs that are hard for predators to see on the rock walls where the spider hunts.

Many spider species look like dead leaves or twigs. The Australian knobbly crab spider has a rough-shaped body whose color is perfectly matched to the tree bark where it hunts small insects. The

Some spiders are able to blend in easily with their sur-roundings.

stick spider imitates a small twig on a tree, and the grass spider blends in perfectly with blades of grass in a field.

Several species of camouflaged spiders can switch colors as needed. The wolf spider of South America can blend in on dark brown tree trunks. If it moves to a gray tree, its color changes to gray within thirty minutes.

Some spiders such as the warty bird-dropping spider look like bird dung. This creature is cov-ered with wrinkles and warts. Its green, shiny skin is flecked with spots of white, giving the strange-looking spider the appearance of clean

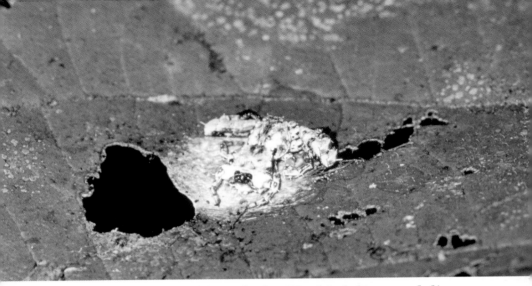

The spider pictured here looks like bird dung and dines on insects attracted to its appearance and odor.

bird droppings. The warty bird dropper sits motionless for days, giving off a manure-smelling scent that repels predators but attracts flies for the spider to eat.

Mimicking Other Insects

Some spiders hide from predators by imitating, or mimicking, other insects. Ants are some of the most common insects in the world. They have very few natural enemies, however, because they have tough shells, taste bad, sting, and attack in large numbers. Since they are usually untouchable, several species of spiders have evolved to look like ants.

Ant spiders that mimic ants live in Brazil, Panama, and Ghana. These spiders not only look like ants but act like them as well. The ant spiders imitate the zigzag pattern of a running ant. Since ants have six legs and constantly wave their antennae, spiders raise their front two legs to mimic ant antennae. Ant spiders live among ants to hide, but they must blend in perfectly or the ants will attack them.

Another species of spider, the *Argiope,* looks like a type of ground-hunting wasp in Uganda. The *Argiope* is protected because birds and other predators fear the sharp stinger of the wasp and mistakenly think that the spider can sting them.

Scorpions are arthropods—members of the spider family—and some spiders mimic scorpions to survive. Predators avoid scorpions because their venom is so poisonous that it can kill large creatures, including humans. When the Australian scorpion spider is disturbed, it raises its

The ant spider's ability to look and act like an ant provides an excellent defense against predators.

abdomen over its head to look like a scorpion. If this trick doesn't work, the spider can tuck its head under and pull in its legs to look like a dead leaf.

The black widow is one of the deadliest spiders, feared by many creatures, including humans. The false black widow spider takes advantage of this situation by mimicking the black widow. The false black widow is identical to the real black widow except that it lacks a red patch hidden on its underside.

Spiders That Attack

When some spiders come under attack, they whirl, jump, twist, and turn to confuse their enemy. Wasps and hummingbirds try to attack several types of web-building spiders such as the daddy long legs. In such a case, the spiders are able to jump up and down so rapidly that their image becomes a blur, confusing the predator.

Other spiders react viciously when attacked. American tarantulas, for instance, are extremely hairy. Their abdomens are covered with sharply barbed hairs that they can shoot at attackers. These hairs are especially painful when shot into the eyes and nose of a predator such as a mouse. They also cause severe itching and inflame the lungs when inhaled. Humans who have been attacked by tarantulas report stinging, itching, and irritation for up to seven days.

The tarantula will react viciously if it is attacked.

The black widow spider is also quick to attack curious mice and other small creatures. When a mouse gets too close, the black widow spins an extremely sticky net from its spinnerets. The spider then jumps on the mouse and pushes the sticky net into its face. Although the web is not poisonous or bitter, the mouse's nose is very sensitive. After one such treatment, the mouse will never bother a black widow again.

Several species of trap-door spiders will rear up on their hind legs when approached by a predator. These spiders expose menacing fangs to scare off enemies. If this doesn't work, the spider will attack, injecting the predator with a strong venom.

The green lynx spider does not even need to attack its enemy. From its fangs, it can spray a bitter, irritating venom into the face of a predator. The spider is tiny—about three-quarters of an inch in size—but it can shoot venom an amazing eight inches, more than ten times its body size. The South American tree-dwelling spiders also

The green lynx spider has the ability to spray venom into a predator's face.

use this type of defense. Instead of spraying venom from their fangs, they spray a nauseating liquid from their abdomen.

Attacking Humans

Some spiders will attack when threatened, but most will simply hide. Very few spiders are aggressive in the face of danger. Fewer still would attack an enemy as large as a human being. Unfortunately, sometimes people will accidentally—or purposely—disturb a spider such as the black widow. Most of the time, black widows will quickly drop out of their webs when approached by a human. But black widows tend to live near humans, in homes and yards. When someone comes too close, the spider will bite. Black widow bites can be very painful, and lead to nausea, dizziness, severe muscle spasms, and even death.

Fortunately, modern medicine has found a cure for the black widow's bite. If the patient is quickly taken to a doctor, he or she can get a shot of anti-venin, a substance that neutralizes the spider's venom.

With their clever instincts and the ability to kill, it is little wonder that spiders have often been shown as monsters in movies or as superheroes like Spiderman in comic books. Spiders live almost everywhere on the planet, from the wild rain forests of South America to the dusty corners of a nearby garage. And while the world constantly changes all around them, spiders continue to hunt, kill, and eat their prey exactly as they have for millions of years.

Glossary

abdomen: The lower segment of a spider's body.

appendage: A body part such as an arm, leg, or tail that is joined to the main body of an animal.

Arthropoda: Phylum, or division, in the animal kingdom that consists of animals with segmented bodies and jointed appendages.

camouflage: The technique of using protective coloring to hide from predators and prey.

carapace: A protective, shell-like covering on a spider's upper body.

carnivores: Animals that eat meat.

cephalothorax: The upper body part of the spider that consists of the joined head and thorax.

enzyme: Juices produced by a spider to break down food sources for digestion.

habitat: The environment in which an organism lives.

palps: Jointed appendages on the spider's head that look like legs but contain sensory organs, also known as pedipalps.

predator: A creature that lives by preying on other organisms.

prey: An animal hunted or caught for food.

species: A category of scientific classification used to label and identify groups of related plants or animals.

spinnerets: Tubular structures from which spiders secrete the silk threads they use to form webs.

thorax: The middle region of the spider's body, between the head and the abdomen, where the legs are attached.

venom: A poisonous secretion made by a spider to paralyze or kill its prey.

For Further Exploration

Jennifer Owings Dewey, *Spiders Near and Far.* New York: Dutton Children's Books, 1993.
> A book about what spiders eat, how they grow, how they spin silk, methods of hunting, and other subjects, written and illustrated by an acclaimed nature author.

Editors of Time-Life Books, *Insects and Spiders.* Alexandria, VA: Time-Life, 1992.
> One of the "Understanding Science and Nature" series for children, this book is full of diagrams, photos, charts, and graphs concerning the bodies, lives, and hunting methods of spiders, bees, locusts, butterflies, and other insects.

Sandra Markle, *Outside and Inside Spiders.* New York: Bradbury Press, 1994.
> Large, color pictures fill out the pages of this informative book about spiders.

Alexandra Parsons, *Amazing Spiders.*
> One of the "Eyewitness Juniors" series, 1990, with photos of huge, hairy spiders, and dozens of fascinating facts about spider hunting, spinning, and habitat.

Dorothy Hinshaw Patent, *Spider Magic.* New York: Holiday House, 1982.
> An easy-to-read book with chapters on all aspects of spiders' lives.

Index